YOUR LAND
AND
MY LAND
AFRICA

We Visit

KENYA

John

Bankston

Mitchell Lane
PUBLISHERS
P.O. Box 196
Hockessin, Delaware 19707

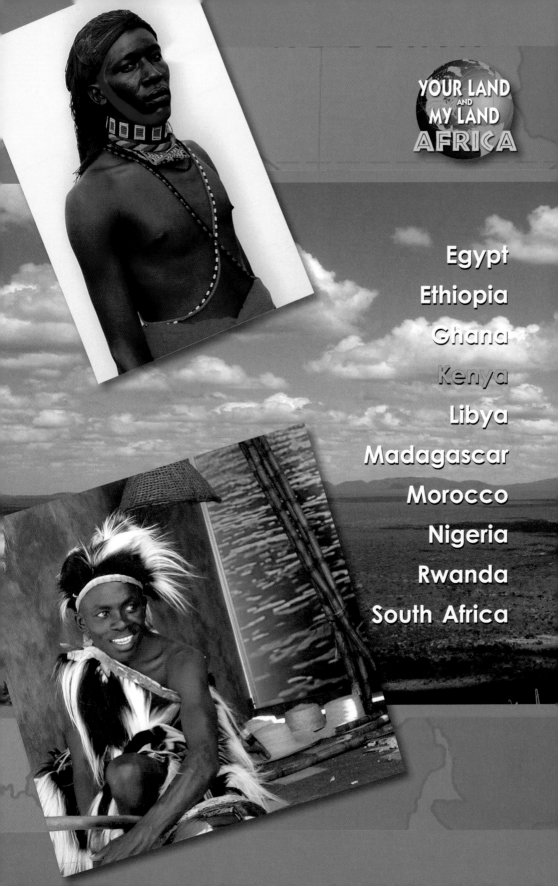

YOUR LAND
AND
MY LAND
AFRICA

Egypt
Ethiopia
Ghana
Kenya
Libya
Madagascar
Morocco
Nigeria
Rwanda
South Africa

LIBYA

EGYPT

Aswān

YOUR LAND
AND
MY LAND
AFRICA

We Visit

KENYA

SUDAN

Addis
Ababa

Mitchell Lane

PUBLISHERS

Printing   1   2   3   4   5   6   7   8   9

Bankston, John, 1974-
  We visit Kenya / by John Bankston.
      p. cm. — (Your land and my land. Africa)
  Includes bibliographical references and index.
  ISBN 978-1-61228-304-3 (library bound)
1. Kenya—Juvenile literature. I. Title. II. Series: Your land and my land (Mitchell Lane Publishers). Africa.
  DT433.522.B35 2012
  967.62—dc23
                                                              2012009623
eBook ISBN: 9781612283784

PUBLISHER'S NOTE: This story is based on the author's extensive research, which he believes to be accurate. Documentation of this research is on page 61.

The internet sites referenced herein were active as of the publication date. Due to the fleeting nature of some websites, we cannot guarantee they will all be active when you are reading this book.

                                                              PLB

Contents

Introduction

Everyone is from Africa. You are from Africa. Your teacher, your neighbor, your best friend—they are all from Africa. It does not matter where you were born, or where your parents were born, or where your great-great-great-great grandparents were born. If you could go back far enough, you would find a distant relation who came from Africa.

How far back? To find out, you could ask a paleontologist—a scientist who studies life in the distant past. Paleontologists focus on fossils—the petrified remains of plants and animals preserved in rock. They have found the oldest human fossils in Africa. The first humans on the entire planet were living in Africa some two million years ago.

These early people were quite different from people today. They were much shorter, for one thing, and hairier. They survived on whatever food they could gather from plants or kill. While they hunted for food, these first humans were also being hunted. But they survived.

Kenya

AFRICA

KENYA

The descendants of those first humans traveled across Asia and Europe and into North and South America.

Today the continent of Africa is made up of fifty-seven independent countries. These borders often change, as sections of countries split off to form their own nations. An election in January of 2011 resulted in the new nation of South Sudan. Forty-seven African colonies, including Kenya, achieved independence from 1950 to 1980.

Bordered by Uganda to the west, South Sudan to the northwest, Ethiopia to the north, Somalia to the northeast, and Tanzania to the south, Kenya also has 333 miles (536 kilometers) of eastern coastline that lies on the Indian Ocean. Kenya, like most African nations, was once a colony. Its people were ruled by Britain, just as the United States once was. And like the U.S., Kenya gained its independence, and today attracts visitors from around the world.

With its long neck and spindly legs, the distinctive giraffe is a Kenyan native and an African icon.

Chapter 1

Land & Life in Kenya

Welcome to Kenya, a country that provides many of the images people around the world have in their minds of Africa. Anyone who has watched a nature documentary or seen a television program featuring lions, zebras, and other animals native to this Eastern African country can picture it. Imagining Kenya means imagining an arid landscape —dry land as far as the eye can see.

This area of Kenya is called the savanna and it receives little rain. But more than the landscape, or the plants, Kenya is known for its animals: giraffes stretching to reach the uppermost leaf of the acacia tree, hippopotamuses lounging contentedly, cheetahs running down their unfortunate prey.

Until the late 19th century, few non-natives had ever ventured past Kenya's thin strip of coastal land along the Indian Ocean. Exploration beyond the coast was challenging. The rivers were difficult to navigate. Worse, the Maasai tribe of southern Kenya had a fearsome reputation. Few wanted to risk an encounter with them.

In the 19th century, a series of unrelated events expanded the outside world's knowledge of Kenya. In the 1840s, two German missionaries named Johann Ludwig Krapf and Johannes Rebmann described the snowcapped mountains they'd seen along the equator of East Africa. Few Europeans believed that snow could actually exist in this area, and most assumed they'd made a mistake. It was not until Scottish explorer Joseph Thomson published a book detailing his 1883-1884 travels across the eastern edge of Lake Victoria and his sighting

Mount Kenya

of Mount Kenya that outsiders began to realize how varied the country's terrain truly was. Thomson's *Through Masai Land* not only described the second-tallest mountain in Africa (Mount Kenya is 17,057 feet, or 5,199 meters high), but also detailed the challenges he faced with the Maasai warriors.

Mount Kenya is located in the Central Highlands of the country. In the Highlands, many live as farmers, and continue the traditions of their ancestors from hundreds, even thousands of years ago. In contrast, to the south of the mountain is Kenya's capital, Nairobi, which resembles many modern cities. Coastal Mombasa is located southeast of Nairobi. This island in the Indian Ocean features both rural villages and four-star resorts.

Lake Victoria lies directly west of Nairobi. One hundred sixty miles (257 kilometers) wide, 210 miles (338 kilometers) long, and 270 feet (82 meters) deep at its center, Lake Victoria is the second-largest lake in the world. It occupies parts of Kenya, Uganda, and Tanzania. Only the aptly-named Lake Superior in North America is larger.

Yet most of Kenya matches expectations. It *is* very dry. Sixty percent of the country receives little rain; much of the country is considered semi-desert. Only 14 percent of the country is suitable for

FYI FACT:

After a giraffe has dined on the acacia tree for a few minutes, the tree secretes a substance that makes its leaves taste terrible—forcing the giraffe to move on. And despite its long neck, the animal has the exact same number of cervical vertebrae as you do: seven!

WHERE IN THE WORLD IS KENYA?

Where in the World

farming. But while the Eastern Plateau, northern plains, and areas along its southern border with Tanzania receive less than 20 inches (51 centimeters) of rain a year, in the Central and Western Highlands some areas see nearly 80 inches (203 centimeters) a year.

Kenya is everything one might imagine. It is also much, much more.

Seen here in 1953 at his Kenyan campsite, author Ernest Hemingway drew inspiration from the country's landscape and wildlife.

A Safari Across Kenya

When people think about Kenya, they often think about safaris. The word comes from Swahili, a native Kenyan language. Swahili was heavily influenced by the Arabic language, as a result of hundreds of years of interactions with Arabic-speaking traders. The word originates from the Arabic *safariya,* meaning "journey." Safari used to mean one thing to Kenya's visitors: hunting. Famous tourists like author Ernest Hemingway, who visited Kenya and popularized the word, often posed for pictures beside the animals they killed. Today people join Kenyan safaris to hunt with cameras. Their only "trophy" is a picture.

For over forty years, tourism has been a primary source of revenue for Kenya—people visiting the country spend money on hotels, food, and safaris. Travelers to Kenya, after dealing with passports, obtaining a visa, and suffering through the recommended shots for malaria, typhoid, hepatitis A, diphtheria, and yellow fever (and booster inoculations for polio and tetanus), generally fly into the country's capital, Nairobi. A modern, urban city of over three million people, it brings with it both a city's advantages and disadvantages. It offers familiar hotel chains and restaurants, but also the threat of street crime that is so common the capital city is often called "Nai-robbery."

Nairobi rests on the southern edge of the Central Highlands, the most densely populated region in Kenya. Parts of this area are forested. Here and along the coast are good places to spot the black-and-white colobus or even the very rare red colobus monkey. Colobus is taken from the Greek word for "mutilated"—unlike other monkeys, these creatures don't have thumbs.

The Central Highlands surround Mount Kenya. The second-highest mountain in Africa (after Mount Kilimanjaro just to the south of Kenya in Tanzania), Mount Kenya is part of an area where elevations are thousands of feet above sea level.

In contrast to the heavily populated Highlands, few people live in the northern portions of Kenya. Most of the region is semi-desert—very dry. Yet it is in the northwest, near Lake Turkana, that fossil evidence from the first human ancestors was discovered. One impressive animal surviving in this harsh environment is the Grevy's zebra, ca-

Weighing in at nearly half-a-ton, the Grevy's Zebra can go five days without a drink of water.

pable of going without water for up to five days. The largest of the three species of zebra, they can weigh nearly 1,000 pounds (450 kilograms) and stand over 5 feet (152 centimeters) tall at the shoulder. Lake Turkana also boasts the largest population of the Nile crocodile in the world. Beginning in the 1940s, two decades of hunting greatly reduced their numbers. Today they number over 20,000 in Lake Turkana alone, since laws have been put in place to protect them. This fearsome reptile kills as many as 300 people every year in Africa.

To the west, the land surrounding Lake Victoria is an area with few outsiders. Here, native Kenyans cultivate the rich farmland and labor on tea plantations which have provided one of the country's main exports for decades. There is even a rainforest, the Kakamega Forest.

Lakes, along with many of the rivers throughout Kenya, are home to the hippopotamus. The hippo can spend up to sixteen hours a day submerged in water. Despite its docile appearance and a weight of up to four tons (3,600 kilograms), it can outrun a person on land. It also secretes a natural protective sunscreen, and eats over 150 pounds (68 kilograms) of vegetation every day. While these facts may be interesting, the most significant fact about hippos is that they are quite dangerous. While guarding their territory, experts believe they kill more people than any other creature in Africa.

Cutting through the northern deserts and the Central Highlands is the Great Rift Valley. Within this trench, and across the surrounding areas, are Kenya's dry grasslands. The flat landscape of the grasslands is interrupted only by acacia trees. Some species of short acacia trees grow near termite mounds, while taller acacia trees are a primary food source for giraffes like the Maasai and the Rothschild.

A visit to Kenya provides numerous opportunities to see wild animals generally only observed in zoos or nature films. Safaris operate in protected preserves where hunting is prohibited. Although tourists can't bring back animal "souvenirs," nearly everyone returns from a Kenyan safari with both pictures and stories. Some of the most popular safaris are in the country's southern region, including the ones at the

Maasai Mara National Reserve. Over a million wildebeest migrate through this reserve every winter in search of food and water, as part of a 300-mile (500-kilometer) annual round trip through Kenya and Tanzania. Visitors here might spot a pride of lions or even a white rhinoceros. Unlike the animals in zoos, the wildlife in these preserves wander freely. Few preserves have fences.

Each year, visitors can enjoy two distinct races. The Rhino Charge is a competition involving dozens of off-road vehicles crossing between thirteen guard posts over a 39-square-mile (100-square-kilometer) course. The location is kept secret before the race and changes every year. Another event with similar entertainment is the Safari Rally. This two-day event takes racers across the savanna to Nairobi.

Although the savanna boasts a great diversity of wildlife, other parts of Kenya offer their own attractions. The dry Maungu Plains separate the country's interior from the coast. Even further, past the shoreline of white sandy beaches, lie coral reefs and islands.

FYI FACT:

Many scientists believe that the hippo is related to the whale.

Shown here fishing in Kenya, the Goliath Heron boasts a wingspan of over 6 feet (182 centimeters). They are the largest living herons in the world.

This is Kenya. It is a country of desert and rainforest, farmland and savanna. It is home to over 300 different species of mammals, over 1,000 species of birds, and over 6,500 different plants.

And while the wildlife here has inspired many travelers to visit, without protection, it is in danger of disappearing sooner rather than later. But some Kenyans have taken action to ensure that Kenya's natural treasures are around for many generations to come.

Born in Kenya to British parents, Joan Root was an Oscar-nominated filmmaker. Her documentaries on Kenyan wildlife and the challenges brought by over-development and poaching reached a global audience. Her outspoken efforts to end illegal hunting and fishing earned her numerous enemies. After her murder in 2006, author Mark Seal published a biography telling her story, called *Wildflower*.

Another Kenyan environmentalist, Wangari Maathai returned to her homeland following her 1966 graduation from college in Pennsylvania. Although she had left only a few years before, she noticed profound changes had occurred since Kenya had achieved independence. With small farmers turning to large commercial crops, mainly tea and coffee, there were fewer crops grown for food. Households were cutting down trees for heat, while expanding farms cleared away trees in favor of crops. Without the roots of trees to keep the soil in place, much of it washed or blew away.

Maathai realized that unless there was a change, her country would quickly face an agricultural crisis. Instead of waiting for the government to solve the problem, she enlisted local women to plant trees. Men, schoolchildren, even soldiers joined her "Green Belt Movement." Some forty million trees have been planted by Kenyans since it began. In 2004, she became the first woman from Africa to win the Nobel Peace Prize.

The son of famous paleoanthropologists, Richard Leakey was in his early twenties when he convinced The National Geographic Society to fund a fossil-finding expedition. He soon found evidence of human ancestors like this hominid skull.

Chapter 3

The Human Cradle

Richard Leakey had a plan. He wanted to lead an expedition along the eastern shore of Kenya's Lake Turkana. Already he had spent several years exploring the border regions of Kenya and Tanzania. Along the edges of the world's largest permanent desert lake, he hoped to find the earliest traces of human existence. He believed that he would find fossil evidence of the first creatures closer to man than to apes preserved in the volcanic rocks.

All Leakey needed was funding—enough money to cover his expenses. The National Geographic Society was his best hope.

Standing before the committee, Leakey was well prepared. He needed to be. He was twenty-three years old. He'd never been to college. He'd led expeditions for his parents, Louis and Mary Leakey, famous paleoanthropologists who studied human fossils. But this time he'd be on his own.

"Taken by his brashness," *Time* magazine later reported, "the committee granted his request. But it came with a warning: 'If you find nothing, you are never to come begging at our door again.'"[1]

Leakey wasn't worried. Today, the area around Lake Turkana is a desert. Millions of years ago, however, it was a tropical rainforest overflowing with plants and animals. The region was also attractive to early humans.

Leading his team in 1968, Richard Leakey knew he had a chance to step out of his father's shadow and prove himself. Like the work his parents had done, his work involved finding evidence of our ancestors who lived thousands, even millions of years ago. There was no better place to find them than central Africa.

The equator traversing the center of Africa has remained a constant over millions of years. Other land masses move. Africa does not. Indeed, the region has changed little over hundreds of millions of years. But the rest of the continents in the world were once connected to Africa. Although today oceans divide them, some 200 million years ago, the continents were a single region called Pangea.

Over millions of years, the land mass separated forming individual continents which eventually moved to their present locations. Africa, however, scarcely moved at all. Some 97 percent of African land has been in place for over 300 million years. This lack of movement, combined with the fact that Kenya is so close to the equator, provided a generally stable climate. The animals and humans that evolved there did not have to face one of the Earth's greatest challenges: winter.

Forces under the earth's crust have a profound impact on its surface. These forces can produce earthquakes or volcanoes, mountains or tidal waves. In most places, plates beneath the earth's crust are pushed together, but in Africa they are stretched apart.

Cutting across Africa, the Great Rift Valley is a deep geological trench widening at the rate of a quarter-inch per year. This process began over thirty million years ago. Eventually, it will split the continent in two. A rich source of fossils, much of the valley lies in Kenya.

Richard Leakey's decision to explore the edges of Lake Turkana was a wise one. His parents had already spent decades searching for fossils to prove their theories about human origins. In a 2011 radio interview, Leakey admitted, "I think I have been very fortunate in my career in that when I went up to Lake Turkana in northern Kenya, it turned out to be there were so many fossils that one really had very little of the difficulties that my parents experienced."[2]

The region itself was challenging—hot and dry; the lake teemed with crocodiles. Yet it did not take long for the expedition to begin making discoveries, assuring the young anthropologist a reputation apart from his well-known parents. One was the nearly intact skull of an australopithecine. His team also found some chopping tools nearby. The skull and the tools came from the same time period, but the tools

FYI FACT:

Although Richard Leakey is known for finding fossils and writing best-selling books about his discoveries, he has also been involved with a number of wildlife projects. In 1989, as head of the Kenya Wildlife Service he worked and fought tirelessly against the ivory trade. When he took over, 100,000 elephants were being killed every year in Africa for their ivory tusks. He armed forest rangers with automatic weapons and "shoot to kill" orders against elephant poachers. Made head of the Kenyan Civil Service in 1999 by President Moi, Leakey hoped to eliminate the agency's corruption. Instead, he was forced to resign from the post less than two years later.

seemed designed for cutting meat, while the australopithecines were vegetarians.

It remains unresolved when the first hominids appeared. Hominid is the name given to the family of primate mammals who walk on two legs. Besides modern man—*Homo sapiens*—it also includes extinct species of *Homo* including *Homo erectus, Homo habilis,* and the extinct genus *Australopithecus.*

Scientists believe our ancestors first stood upright over three million years ago. From there, the genus *Homo* emerged. Short, squat, and covered in hair, they looked more ape than human. But they were evolving.

Evolution is the theory that over thousands, even millions of years, genetic mutations give an animal's offspring advantages over others in their species. These advantages allow the changed animals to live longer and reproduce in larger numbers than the unchanged animals. Eventually, the changes are so profound that a new species is created.

The region of Africa where Kenya is located offers visual evidence of these changes. Evolution is how giraffes came to have long necks, and why cheetahs can run in short bursts of speed close to 70 miles per hour (113 kilometers per hour). The evidence is also seen in fossils, the preserved remains of creatures who walked the earth millions of years ago.

Much of what makes us human developed in Africa. As author John Reader notes in *Africa*, "All our distinctive characteristics—our ability to walk on two legs for long distances; our hands, with an opposable forefinger and thumb able to perform delicate tasks; our bare skin; sweating; and our brain—were all adaptations that evolved in response to the demands of the savanna environment."[3]

Humans and chimpanzees share 98% of the same DNA—the building block of life. Sometime between five and seven million years ago, we shared a common ancestor with chimpanzees. This ancestor most likely lived somewhere just to the west of the Rift Valley, in an area that was then covered in forests. The descendants of this common ancestor split into two groups: one branch became human; the other became modern apes. "It is as though a magician had drawn a veil over the scene, then ushered forth the bipedal [two-footed] ancestor of humanity," notes John Reader.[4]

Walking upright on two feet is fairly unique. As Reader explains, it requires a great deal of energy. In order to carry the weight of the upper body upon the legs, the head shifted and was carried atop the backbone which developed curves in the neck and lower spine. Among other changes, the arms shortened and the feet lost their ability to grasp.

Most scientists believe these changes happened fairly quickly. After all, an animal would have a hard time walking on both four legs and two. At the moment, there are no known fossils of such a creature.

Because of the lack of evidence, some suggest evolutionary theory is inaccurate. At a May 2011 conference in New York's American Museum of Natural History, Leakey's rival paleoanthropologist Donald C. Johanson gave his opinion on the theory that has been the basis of his life's work. "Evolution is a fact," he offered. "It is the best explanation of what is known from observations. It is a theory as powerful as the theory of gravity."[5]

Nearly forty years before, Leakey was certain his assistant had discovered the missing piece of the evolutionary puzzle. In 1972, Bernard Ngeneo found fragments of a skull. The discovery—called 1470 after its catalog number at the Nairobi National Museum—was identified as *Homo habilis* or "handy man." It may have been the first member of our own genus. Genus is the classification between the

Dr. Richard Leakey

family and the species. This creature had quite a bit in common with our own species, *Homo sapiens.*

Forty years ago, modern man was viewed as the product of an unbroken line from the *Australopithecus* to *Homo habilis, Homo erectus,* and finally *Homo sapiens.* Ngeneo's discovery provided an alternate theory.

Homo habilis's cranial capacity was almost twice the size of the *Australopithecus* and was considered more intelligent. This supported the theory of man's development—if *Australopithecus* was followed by the more intelligent *Homo habilis.* There was only one problem. The skull was believed to be over two million years old. It would have existed at the exact same time as many *Australopithecus* hominids.

"It all gets very technical," Leakey admitted in 2011, "but one of the problems with paleoanthropology is that although there's a remarkable story, much of the story is still represented by frustratingly fragmentary evidence. And so more has to be found to tie up a few loose ends."[6]

Not everyone agreed with Leakey's conclusion. In bordering Ethiopia, Donald Johanson's discovery of fossils nicknamed "Lucy" and the "First Family" led him to a different conclusion. He believed those

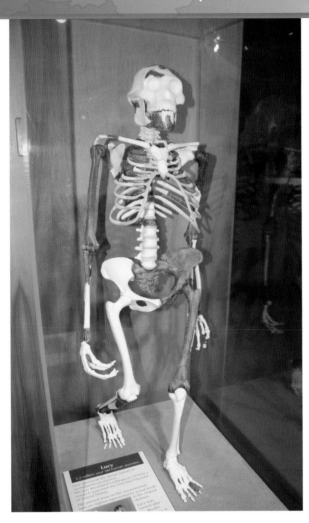

Nicknamed "Lucy," this *Australopithecus afarensis* skeleton is displayed at the Cleveland Natural History Museum. Donald Johanson believed it disproved Richard Leakey's theories about our early ancestors.

fossils—which he called a new species, *Australopithecus afarensis*—pre-dated both *Homo habilis* and later versions of *Australopithecus.*

Today, many scientists believe that Leakey's 1470 is not *Homo habilis* at all, but is instead a completely different species, *Homo rudolfensis.* Modern dating techniques have shown that the skull is probably closer to 1.9 million years old. This new estimate means that a human descent from *Australopithecus* can't yet be ruled out. Although the debate between Leakey, Johanson, and their respective supporters remains unresolved, most scientists agree about one aspect of human origins. The earliest humans lived in Africa, many of them in the area now known as Kenya.

KENYA FACTS AT A GLANCE

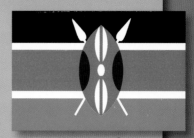

Kenyan flag

Full name: Republic of Kenya

Official languages: English, Swahili

Population: 43,013,341 (July 2012 estimate)

Land area: 219,746 square miles (569,140 square kilometers); roughly twice the size of Nevada.

Capital: Nairobi

Government: Republic

Ethnic makeup: Kikuyu 22%, Luhya 14%, Luo 13%, Kalenjin 12%, Kamba 11%, Kisii 6%, Meru 6%, other African 15%, non-African (Asian, European, and Arab) 1%

Religions: Protestant 45%, Roman Catholic 33%, Muslim 10%, indigenous beliefs 10%, other 2% (note: percentages are estimates)

Exports: Tea, coffee, fish, petroleum products

Imports: Machinery and transportation equipment, motor vehicles, petroleum products, iron and steel, plastics

Crops: Tea, coffee, corn, wheat, sugarcane, fruit, vegetables

Average high temperatures:
  Mombasa: February 91°F (33°C); August 83°F (28°C)
  Nairobi: February 80°F (27°C); July 71°F (22°C)

Average annual rainfall:
  Mombasa: 43 inches (109 centimeters)
  Nairobi: 38 inches (96 centimeters)
  Most of Kenya receives less than the 29.5 inches (74.3 centimeters) of rainfall per year that is considered the minimum needed for subsistence farming. In the central and western highlands, however, average annual rainfall exceeds 30 inches (76 centimeters) and can reach 70 inches (178 centimeters). Most of Kenya has two rainy seasons, from March to May and October to December.

Highest point: Mount Kenya, 17,057 feet (5,199 meters)

Longest river: Tana River, flowing 440 miles (708 kilometers)

Flag: Three equal horizontal bands of black (top), red, and green; the red band is edged in white; a large Maasai warrior's shield covering crossed spears is superimposed at the center; black symbolizes the majority population, red the blood shed in the struggle for freedom, green stands for natural wealth, and white for peace; the shield and crossed spears symbolize the defense of freedom.

National anthem: "Ee Mungu Nguvu Yetu" ("Oh God of All Creation")

National flower: None, although many consider the tropical orchid the unofficial national flower.

National bird: The Lilac-Breasted Roller

National tree: Umbrella Acacia Tree

Source: *CIA World Factbook: Kenya*

On April 18, 2001, when Kenyan Geoffrey Mutai crossed the Boston Marathon's finish line, he did more than win the race. He also ran a marathon faster than anyone else in the world.

Chapter 4

Marathons Around Mount Kenya

On a cold spring day in 2011, a Kenyan ran the fastest marathon ever on one of the toughest courses in the world. It was April 18—a Monday—when Geoffrey Mutai crossed the finish line of the Boston Marathon with a time of two hours, three minutes, and two seconds. No one had ever run the 26.2 miles (42.4 kilometers) in less time.

The Boston Marathon is an elite event. Across the world, tens of thousands compete just to qualify. On race day, over 20,000 runners line up in the late morning hours while half-a-million spectators wait for them to race through the city's center. During the final third, a series of hills challenges even the best of the competitors.

Beginning in the Newton suburb, the four hills conclude after mile twenty. The incline is less than half-a-mile. It would not be so daunting, except for two things. Until the hills, much of the race is slightly downhill. And by the twentieth mile, runners are already near exhaustion. Racers defeated by its geography call the incline "Heartbreak Hill."

Winning a total of $225,000, Mutai overcame Heartbreak Hill but could not overcome the International Association of Athletics Federations (IAAF). The organization refused to certify his time as a world record because the Boston Marathon did not meet its requirements for start/finish separation and elevation. Mutai disagreed. The "Boston Marathon does not have an easy course... In fact, it is tougher than other courses I have competed in," the Kenyan argued.[1]

Margaret Okayo in London

Despite not certifying the race, the IAAF acknowledged that Mutai had run the fastest marathon in the world. He was not the first Kenyan to set a marathon record in Boston. In 2002, fellow Kenyan Margaret Okayo set a record for women, completing the race in two hours, twenty minutes, and forty-three seconds. A Kenyan has won the men's race six out of the last seven times (2006-2012) and nineteen out of the last twenty-two (1991-2012).

Kenyan runners don't just win marathons. They've been besting competitors in races across the world for over forty years. In the 1968 Olympics, Kip Keino collapsed during the 10,000 meters. Suffering from a gallbladder infection, he ignored doctor's orders and continued to compete, defeating world-record-holder Jim Ryun in the 1,500 meters.

A long distance runner, in 1972 Keino became the only man to hold Olympic records at two distances. Winner of a gold medal in the 1968 Olympics, he continues to promote the sport as chairman of the Kenyan Olympic Committee. When he was a young child, both of his parents died, motivating his ongoing work with orphans today. Named one of *Sports Illustrated* magazine's "Sportsmen of the Year" in 1987, today he and his wife run farms and educate and care for orphans.

Currently Kenyan men hold seven of the ten fastest recorded times in the marathon and six of the top ten in the half marathon. Kenyan women do well, also. They have two of the ten fastest times in the marathon and thirteen of the top twenty in the half marathon. And of the top 400 fastest marathons, well over 100 title holders are Kenyan.[2]

For so many top runners to come out of a single country would be remarkable enough. But the runners don't just come from Kenya. Many of them come from a single tribe—the Kalenjin.

Numbering some three million members, the Kalenjin have also been political leaders in Kenya. As runners, they are unmatched. People have been trying to figure out why for decades. Some point to the elevation of their homeland—most live in the highlands of Kenya. At high altitudes, the air pressure is lower, and less oxygen is inhaled with every breath. To compensate, more red blood cells are produced to deliver the oxygen throughout the body. Because runners who have lived in high-altitude environments can get oxygen to their muscles more efficiently, they are faster and have more endurance when they compete at lower altitudes. Others point to a diet rich in meat, milk, and starches, or the relative poverty in Kenya where prize money is a great motivator.

Yet those factors alone may not be enough. Recently, as part of a controversial television program on Britain's Channel 4, Danish scientists pitted randomly selected Danes against randomly selected Kalenjin. All of them were untrained. After three months of identical training, the Kalenjin teens easily beat the Danes. The scientists pointed to physical differences between the boys, noting that the Kalenjin had "birdlike legs, very long levers which are very, very thin" allowing them to "bounce and skip" over the course. While the Kenyan athletes "flowed through the running motion," the Danes "landed heavily and sunk into the ground and almost had to pull themselves forward."[3]

Physical differences are connected to evolution and successful genetic mutations. The Kalenjin were a Nilotic people who traveled south from the Nile River. The group raised cattle; some have suggested the fastest captured the most cattle from rival tribes. Possessing a large number of cattle, in this tribe, also meant being able to marry multiple wives and thus have more children. These children may have inherited their fathers' speed.

FYI FACT:

Like runners from Kenya, marathons have a lengthy history. The name itself dates to a battle and a legend. In 492 B.C.E., Greeks who had made their home in Ionia rose up against their Persian rulers. Two years later, they faced the Persian army at the town of Marathon. Although mainland Greeks joined their Ionian countrymen, they were still outnumbered by the Persian army. Ten thousand Greeks faced some 25,000 Persians. By encircling the enemy, the Greeks beat the odds and won their first victory in the war.

According to legend, the Greeks enlisted a messenger to bring the news of their victory at Marathon to military leaders in Athens. Pheidippides ran the 26-mile (42-kilometer) distance and dropped dead from exhaustion moments after delivering the momentous news. Although the story is not based in fact, it inspired the modern 26-mile contest.

At a Kenyan National Park, a cheetah is captured running at full speed.

The idea that genetic advantages are why Kalenjin win races has been dismissed as racist by Keino. He believes they win because of hard work. Still, in ancient Kenya, running was a means of survival, not competition. Death was often the penalty for the slowest. Some of the fastest animals in the world live in the region; thousands of years ago human beings were part of their menu.

Human beings are not the strongest animal, nor the fastest. Despite evolving to be one of the smartest creatures on earth, thousands of years ago their survival skills were limited. To compensate, they developed endurance. A cheetah, for example, can only run at nearly 70 miles per hour (113 kilometers per hour) for less than a minute.

What humans can do—better than their primate cousins, better than most mammals—is run for long distances over long periods of time. This is endurance. Many scientists believe it was one of the traits of our early evolution. Chasing down their next meal, early humans overwhelmed exhausted animals. This was a tremendous advantage. Those who ran the best, probably lived the longest.

Today, runners from all over the world can train like the Kalenjin. The High Altitude Training Centre in Iten, Kenya, provides meals, personal training, and the chance to run for fifteen days at some 8,000 feet (2,400 meters) above sea level—all for less than $1,500 U.S. dollars.

Numerous museums are scattered across Kenya, including this one—the Kenya Railway Museum. It offers visitors a look at how trains affected life in Kenya.

Migrations Along the Rift

Visitors to another country often wonder about the best way to learn its history. They might read a book or visit a museum. You would expect a country with as long a history as Kenya to have great museums. It does.

There are museums that showcase the country's artists, and the Karen Blixen Museum which is devoted to *Out of Africa's* author. There's even a railway museum, with authentic engines from the country's first rail line. Yet the most popular attractions are probably those dedicated to pre-historic Kenya.

The Reverend Harry Leakey, grandfather of famous paleoanthropologist Richard Leakey, was one of the Nairobi Natural History Museum's founders in 1910. Over three decades later, Harry's son Louis began working as its curator. He did more than just contribute many of the museum's fossils. He also abolished its "whites only" admission policy (a decade before similar rules were outlawed in the United States).

Renamed the Nairobi National Museum in 2008, today the Museum Hill location features the Prehistory Gallery. Just a thirty-minute walk from Nairobi's city center, Richard Leakey continued his family's legacy here. Besides being the home of 1470—the skull at the center of the debate over human origins—the gallery offers visitors the chance to see skulls of apes, hominids, fossilized footprints and life-sized displays of how our ancestors looked millions of years ago.

While some stick to museums, more adventuresome travelers explore ruins or venture into churches and fortresses. In Kenya, these opportunities are all available.

Over three days in March, Nairobi hosts the East African Art Festival. Organized by Kenya's National Museums, the festival offers visitors a variety of entertainment covering everything from film and literature to dance and the visual arts. Yet the best way for visitors to learn about this country's history is to learn about its present. Kenya's history is more than just artifacts. The history of Kenya is seen in the way Kenyans live. It is seen in the food they eat and how they earn a living, in the art they create and in their family customs.

Today it is estimated that there are more than forty traditional ethnic groups in Kenya. These groups are often called "tribes." Tribes have a common language and history, they have different customs and traditions than other tribes. The histories of some Kenyan tribes stretch back thousands of years.

The 21st century has affected the way many Kenyans live and the customs they practice. But despite Nairobi's modern skyscrapers, many Kenyans live in small homes with thatched roofs—a covering made of grass or straw. In the countryside, these are often huts made of mud

Nairobi

with dirt floors. Even in Nairobi, there are poorer areas where such construction is common.

Contact with the West—with both European colonists and travelers from places like the U.S.—has influenced the way many Kenyans dress, especially in urban areas. Outside of the cities, the way Kenyans dress varies from tribe to tribe. In some areas, traditional, rural women may wear a kanga—a brightly colored, one-piece cotton garment—but many people in Kenya dress in fashions similar to those worn by visitors.

Still, modern life includes some ancient traditions. In many tribes, for example, a groom's family would give the bride's family cattle or other livestock as payment for the loss of her labor. Today, the Kikuyu tribe still practices this "bridewealth" custom. Instead of animals, however, many are now asking for cash.

Tribal rivalries sometimes lead to violence. Only a few decades ago, these conflicts were settled with traditional weapons, like spears. Today, combatants might use guns, as well.

But in many ways, thousands of Kenyans live much as their ancestors did. The beginnings of human history stretch back to the hunter-gatherers. Many occupied the fertile Central Highlands northwest of the modern city of Nairobi. In one article, anthropologists explained that hunter-gatherers "had sole dominion over the continent for millennia before the advent of agriculture, the Bantu expansion, and the rise of the great kingdoms of the savannah and Sudan. Africa is the cradle of humankind, and ninety percent of human history—in Africa and elsewhere—is the history of hunting and gathering."[1]

Hunting and gathering is the most primitive of survival techniques. It means following the food and relying on chance. Small groups of hunter-gatherers were often made up of a single family; the work was usually divided by gender. The men would hunt, the women would gather. The men chased down animals while the women picked whatever grew in the wild.

There is some debate about whether or not descendants of the first hunter-gatherers still exist in remote areas of Kenya. Some tribes possibly connected to those first hunter-gatherers include the Boni and the Sengwer. In the 21st century, there are an estimated 400,000 hunter-gatherers in Africa. Large numbers of them live in Kenya, including the Okiek, a Rift Valley forest tribe, the Dahalo along the coast, and the Waata who reside beside the Tana River at the country's border with Somalia.

Many of these tribes are struggling. This is not due to a lack of food, but because the land they once relied upon has been taken by the government for wildlife preserves or sold for farmland. As a result, tribes like the Okiek who live in the forests of central Kenya, have largely abandoned hunting and gathering in favor of farming.

If food became scarce in one area, hunter-gatherers traveled to new locations. Migration—moving from one area to another—is the normal pattern for human existence. This movement of early humans not only populated Africa, but the rest of the world.

There are varying theories regarding the human migration from Africa to the rest of the world. The most widely accepted theory involves a small band of humans crossing through the Red Sea into Asia. They were tall and slender, with short faces and high foreheads unmarked by distinctive brow ridges like those of *Homo habilis* and *Homo erectus.* These people were *Homo sapiens* or "wise man"—they were some of the first people. The group was small, between 100 and 1,000 men, women, and children. According to this theory, it is from this group that many modern humans can trace their background.

Before modern roads, travelers relied on natural pathways. The Kyber Pass cutting through the Spin Ghar Mountains was for thousands of years the primary means of crossing between Northern and Southern Asia. Many anthropologists believe the Bering Strait allowed the first settlers to reach North America. And in Africa, the main north-south route was provided by the Great Rift Valley.

The first significant migrations within Africa came from groups who abandoned the uncertainty of hunter-gatherer lives for the more reliable methods of raising animals and farming. Beginning around

Great Rift Valley

2000 B.C.E., these groups began arriving in what is modern Kenya, traveling along the Great Rift Valley—Kenya's first "highway."

In Kenya, the period from 500 B.C.E. to 500 C.E. marked a steady migration of settlers from surrounding regions. Today, most people in Kenya are related to one of the three core groups who populated Kenya —the Cushites, the Nilotes, and the Bantus. Because members of each group often married members from the other ones, many Kenyans are related to more than just one group. Each group has a distinctive language and culture; today Bantu peoples make up the majority of Kenyans.

The Cushites were the first group in Kenya, arriving from Ethiopia some 4,000 years ago. They introduced farming to Kenya, raising cereals like millet and sorghum. They also raised cattle who grazed on grasslands in areas where farming was impossible.

Cushites crafted arrowheads and axes from obsidian, a dark volcanic glass that forms after lava cools. Remains of their early settlements have been found in Hyrax Hill near Nakuru. One of their most significant achievements still endures.

Obsidian arrowhead

The Cushites built elaborate irrigation systems to provide water for their farms. Today, one of these systems is not just an artifact—it is still in use just west of Lake Baringo, in the Elgeyo Escarpment.

By 1000 B.C.E., Cushites traveling from Somalia settled in Western Kenya and the Highlands. Other Cushitic settlers left the Ethiopian Highlands after 1300 C.E., arriving in northeastern Kenya.

Although western and southern Cushites were absorbed by the later Bantu and Nilotic cultures, or driven out of the area, in the north they maintained a distinct culture. Today they are the only Cushitic-speaking group in Kenya. They still live a nomadic lifestyle. Numbering less than one million, their herds graze around Lake Turkana. Many float on palm rafts in the lake, using harpoons to spear fish, just as their ancestors did hundreds of years ago.

Kenya is a sub-Saharan country—it lies south of the Sahara desert. Thousands of years ago, the Nilotes left the Nile River region in search of a better place to raise their livestock. Arriving in Kenya at varying times, the Nilotes were animal herders who considered themselves superior to farmers. Crossing into what is now Kenya, they may have conquered the hunter-gatherers already living in the western part of the country.

From the original migrations, three distinct cultures arose, based upon where the Nilotes settled—Plains Nilotes, River-Lake Nilotes and Highland Nilotes. The Highland Nilotes are the ancestors of the Kalenjin people, who are very active in politics. The notorious and fierce Maasai are descendants of those first Plains Nilotes.

Visitors to modern Kenya probably find their encounters with the Maasai the most memorable. Maasai can often be seen at Kenya's markets, selling crafts to tourists by day and performing traditional dances at night. Of all of the ethnic groups living in 21st century Kenya, they have perhaps the most distinctive adornments.

Celebrating the training of a *moran,* or warrior, their celebratory processions are an opportunity to witness their elaborate decorations. Male celebrants wear tiny braids in their hair, colored with ochre—a clay that is one of the oldest pigments in the world. Garbed in red cloth around their waists and beads around their necks, each warrior carries a spear. Women walk beside them, wearing long, oval ornaments stretching their ears and handcrafted, oversized beaded collars.

Bantu ancestors originally settled in the dense forests between the Congo and Niger Rivers. Migrating across the forest land, they reached the grasslands of East Africa around 500 B.C.E. They brought with them the tools of a new age, the Iron Age.

This was the first group to use iron tools for farming, clearing the forest and plowing the fields. Their tools were more efficient; their farms thrived. Their initial success is one reason that they are the dominant group today. In the southwest and center of the country are Bantu groups such as the Meru, the Kamba, and the Kikuyu. The Kikuyu settled around Mount Kenya and the fertile Central Highlands, growing a variety of crops and trading regularly with the Maasai.

Although today some Kikuyu produce goods including coffee and tea, many have settled in urban areas like Nairobi. Often well-educated, they have adopted numerous aspects of 21st century life, including cell phones and computers. Representing the largest tribe in Kenya, over 20 percent of the population is Kikuyu.

 The second-largest city in Kenya, coastal Mombasa offers a different climate and way of life than the rest of the country.

Mombasa:
The Place of War

Imagine diving beneath the lukewarm waters of the Indian Ocean, exploring ancient wrecks along a stretch of the prettiest coral reefs on the planet. Or strolling through a traditional Muslim community, marked by the minarets of mosques signifying over one thousand years of Islamic presence. Picture wandering among the ruins and forts, standing as symbols of the first time European feet touched the white sandy seashore. It is a place with resorts and stretches of modern development, but also slightly seedy campsites and cottages enjoyed by backpackers and budget tourists. After a tiring day of exploring, numerous juice bars offer a wide variety of drinks with ingredients ranging from mangos to beets.

All of these experiences are possible in and around Mombasa, the second-largest city in Kenya. An island, it connects to the mainland by bridges, causeways, and a ferry to the south. Guidebooks often recommend exploring the area on foot. It is, after all, how many people got around the island hundreds of years ago.

In November, visitors and locals alike enjoy the Mombasa Carnival. Not just a simple parade, this festival features floats which depict all of the major cultures and religions across the country. Traditional music and dances are also enjoyed by visitors who are able to satisfy their appetites at the numerous food stalls set up across the city.

Unlike the interior regions, the climate along the eastern coast of Africa has remained unchanged for over 30 million years. The Indian Ocean has remained warm and tropical. Thousands of years ago, the climate provided consistent harvests for farmers and reliable weather for settlers. Life was also affected by monsoons—winds that could destroy, but also provided opportunities. It was on these winds that the first traders arrived, traveling on wooden dhows.

Piloting these small sailing boats from India, China, and the Middle East, they were the first people from the outside world to reach East Africa. By 150 C.E., the Roman geographer Ptolemy began mapping the Kenyan coast. In the first century C.E., Arabs began trading with native Kenyans. Their power did not extend inland, however. Past the Maungu Plains, the Arabs relied on their connections with various coastal tribes. Groups like the Kamba (a Bantu ethnic group) traded a variety of desirable goods, including ivory. Although mainly used for decoration and ceremonies by Kenyans, ivory was a highly sought-after commodity outside of the country. The ivory trade cost thousands of elephants their lives.

Along with ivory, Kenyans brought the Arabs leopard skins and poles made from mangrove trees, while Arabs provided silk, salt, beads, and other items not readily available in Kenya. The Arabs also imported their religion.

Following the death of the prophet Muhammad in 632 C.E., the Islamic faith spread across much of Africa. Rivalries between two sects led many Arabs to leave their homelands. When they reached coastal Kenya, many of them married natives which led to widespread adoption of their religion. It was this combining of cultures which produced a brand new one—Swahili, or "people of the coast." Today, some 10 percent of Kenyans are Muslim, while 78 percent identify with various Christian faiths.

Historians estimate that Mombasa was founded around 900 C.E. By the 12th century, the 6-square-mile (15-square-kilometer) island was a favored trading destination. Today it's the largest port in East Africa.

By the time of the city's founding, trade routes along the Indian Ocean had been bringing goods to the coast of Kenya for centuries. Outbound ships were packed with ivory, cattle, and other local products. Soon, the cargo included humans as well.

Succeeding where Columbus had failed, Vasco da Gama was the first European to find a sea route to India.

Trade was a primary motivator of the sailing son of a Portuguese governor. Vasco da Gama had one goal. He wanted to discover a new route to India. Unlike Christopher Columbus, who wound up off the coast of what would become the United States of America, da Gama succeeded.

Traveling south along the western shores of Africa, da Gama and the four naval ships under his command reached the Cape of Good Hope in 1497. From there, the ships headed north to Mombasa. Local leaders in Mombasa sent large quantities of oranges, spices, and even a sheep. The Portuguese could only offer a string of coral beads.

As soon as he returned to Portugal, da Gama described the wonders he'd witnessed and the wealthy, well-developed cities along the west coast. Unfortunately, the Portuguese differed from traders Kenyans had encountered before. They were interested in conquest, not commerce. When Portuguese ships returned to Mombasa, they were heavily armed and demanded payment. Those who refused were attacked.

Across Africa, the communities were disconnected, their leaders unwilling or unable to ally against the invaders. Town after town quickly fell under the onslaught. But in Mombasa, bands of Arabs and Swahili repelled the invasion.

On three separate occasions, the city was nearly destroyed. The first two attacks, in 1505 and 1528, were unsuccessful. Finally, in 1589 —nearly 100 years after da Gama's explorations—the Portuguese overwhelmed the defenders of Mombasa. Ultimately, the dedication of the natives was no match for the Europeans' superior numbers. Although the Portuguese had little interest in colonizing Kenya or developing a territory ruled from afar, they wanted to use the port of Mombasa for the trade in ivory and as a route to India. The Portuguese also introduced new crops including corn and potatoes.

Today Fort Jesus remains as a monument to the Portuguese victory, as well as evidence of the concerns of Kenya's new residents. For only with the protection of a fortress could they hope to stay in power there.

FYI FACT:

Construction of Fort Jesus began in 1593, designed by Italian architect Giovanni Battista Cairati. It was constructed on a coral ridge at the entrance to Mombasa Harbor. Today it is operated as a museum.

Branding slaves for trade

The Portuguese slowly lost interest in East Africa, favoring the western end of the continent. There, they had begun trading for gold with the Akan states in what is now southern Ghana. The tribes there had little interest in Portuguese goods. Instead, the Portuguese paid for gold with human currency: slaves brought from other parts of Africa. The tribes used theses slaves to mine gold when they couldn't get enough local labor to keep up with the demand.

Even before da Gama landed in Mombasa, slaves were shipped from Africa to Portugal. On August 8, 1444, the first ones reached the country. Describing the scene, the royal librarian wrote: "What heart could be so hard as to not be pierced with piteous feeling to see that company? For some kept their heads low and their faces bathed in tears."[1]

Over two centuries of rule, the Portuguese traded in human cargo. Slaves were not only traded for gold, they were also shipped back to Portugal, and eventually the Americas. Kenyan slaves were often taken to Zanzibar and shipped as far away as India and China. By the middle of the 19th century, when the trans-Atlantic slave trade was abolished, over eleven million slaves had been brought across the ocean to North and South America.

Beginning in 1660, the Omanis—Arabs who ruled from nearby Muscat—fought for control of Mombasa. By 1729, they had finally overthrown the Portuguese. For over a century, the trading port of Mombasa was under Arab control. Then, another European power became interested in Kenya.

European leaders attending the Berlin Conference in 1884 meet to divide Africa into colonies.

Chapter 7

Colonized

In 1884 and 1885, European countries attending the Berlin Conference divvied up Africa like children choosing marbles. The continent itself was unrepresented—African natives were not asked how they felt about the divisions. Instead, territories were crafted without any consideration for tribal boundaries. Border lines divided tribal territory or included rival tribes in one area.

The conference wasn't meant to help Africans. It was designed to benefit European countries who hoped to develop Africa—countries that had "discovered" a region populated by human beings thousands of years before they ever reached Europe.

After Portugal ceded control of Mombasa, the region was run by Arab rulers called sultans. By the early 1840s, Sultan Sayyid Said ruled much of coastal East Africa from Zanzibar. With the Sultan's permission, missionaries entered mainland Kenya. They weren't interested in commerce or conquest—their goal was conversion.

Hoping to convert inland natives to Christianity, missionaries risked disease and death at the hands of aggressive tribes. In 1849, Germans Johann Ludwig Krapf and Johannes Rebmann of the Church Missionary Society became the first Europeans to spot Mount Kenya, which gave the country its name. Their descriptions inspired explorers like Joseph Thomson, who in the 1880s described his encounters with a native tribe in the book, *Through Masai Land*.

The Maasai controlled the ivory trade soon after they reached Kenya. They were also known for their fierce resistance to slavery—most slavers were afraid of them.

The experiences of missionaries and explorers in the 19th century fueled European interest in the area. In 1887, Zanzibar's Sultan Barghash leased his mainland territories, including Kenya, to the British East Africa Association. Hoping to profit from control of the new land, the company lost a fortune, and soon went broke.

In 1893, under orders from the British Prime Minister, Sir Gerald Portal explored Kenya. Finding few humans living between the coastal plain and Lake Victoria, Portal described an agricultural paradise that "would appear to offer every inducement to the European colonist were it not for the presence in the neighbourhood of the warlike and predatory Maasai."[1]

By the time of his report, the dangers from the Maasai were greatly diminished as rinderpest and bovine pleuropneumonia had decimated their cattle herds, while a smallpox epidemic killed off many in the tribe. In 1895, the British government took over control of the country from the British East Africa Association. Although Kenya's coastline had profitable ports, Britain viewed the interior as nothing more than a connection to Uganda. This British territory had already proven its potential. Kenya was an obstacle.

Under the new British East Africa Protectorate, the government set about constructing a railroad linking Mombasa with Lake Victoria. Critics called it "The Lunatic Express."

Natives were offered jobs constructing the railroad, but few were interested. They traded goods and had little use for money. So, labor was imported from India, another British colony. Indians suffered greatly during the railroad's construction and hundreds of them died from injury and disease.

Completed in less than ten years, the railroad stretched 300 miles (482 kilometers) from Mombasa to Nairobi, and then another 215 miles (347 kilometers) to Lake Victoria before entering Uganda. It opened up the interior of Kenya for both exploration and opportunity.

White settlers from Britain began running plantations growing everything from tea and coffee to tobacco. Many of them became very wealthy.

In 1906, the British Government established the Legislative Council, which first met in 1907. This organization formed Kenya's government. Made up exclusively of white British settlers, it generally passed rules favoring those expatriates over native Kenyans. In 1915, the Crown Lands Ordinance made it illegal for anyone other than a white settler to own land in Kenya. By then, natives finally had a use for money. The British were taxing them.

Fighting in two world wars drew Britain's attention away from Kenya. In both conflicts Kenyans were conscripted—forced to fight for Britain in Africa and in other parts of the world. In 1920, the country was officially re-named the Kenya Colony and Protectorate.

During this period, Kenyans began to oppose British taxes and the takeover of their native lands. Founded in 1921 by Harry Thuku, the Young Kikuyu Association was the first formal group opposing British rule. Educated and employed in a Nairobi government job, Thuku inspired a protest when he was arrested. During that protest, more than twenty strikers were killed.

Reorganized in 1924 as the Kikuyu Central Association, the KCA's goals were the same as the goals of the original group. Five years later the head of the KCA, Jomo Kenyatta, asked the British Parliament to allow an elected native representative to serve on the Legislative Council. He was refused.

In 1939, Britain became embroiled in World War II. The country was changed by the war. Devastated by bombings and other attacks, Britain lacked the money to properly administer her colonies. Into this void stepped a movement in Kenya more deadly than all the others. Natives' dreams of independence would come true, but not before hundreds died in a campaign of terror.

Enraged after native-owned land was given to white settlers, Mau Mau rebels battled British rule during the 1950s. Here, a group of Mau Mau is guarded by British soldiers.

Chapter

8

Independence!

In the 19th century, it was often said that, "the sun never sets on the British empire." With territories from Australia to Canada, it was always daytime in at least one country under British rule. But by the middle of the 20th century, twilight was fast approaching.

After World War II, Britain focused on problems at home. During the war, their military had fought on multiple fronts, many halfway around the globe. German bombs had damaged much of London. The money they had spent on the war left them unable to tend to their colonies.

Starting in the early 1900s, countries under British rule including Ireland and India became independent. In the 1950s, the Kenyans' anger toward Britain exploded. A group called the Mau Mau was formed by members of the Kikuyu tribe. They banded together after their most fertile land was given to white settlers. Many of them had fought in World War II. They were well-trained and comfortable with weapons. Beginning in 1952, the group attacked British supporters from their base in the forests surrounding Mount Kenya.

Arresting Mau Mau leader Jomo Kenyatta, Britain declared a state of emergency and began a four-year war against the group. During the conflict, thirty-two Europeans and tens of thousands of Africans were killed. But the Kenyan people gained a number of important freedoms. In 1957, Africans could be elected to the Legislative Council for the first time; two years later they were allowed to settle in the region known as the "White Highlands."

Jomo Kenyatta rides through the streets of Nairobi as Kenya's newly elected Prime Minister on June 1, 1963. This day marked the official start of self-government in Kenya; today June 1 is called Madaraka Day and is celebrated each year in Kenya.

The group considered by many to be a terrorist organization was not the only reason Kenya was granted independence in 1963. By then, Britain faced a native population increasingly willing to fight for their rights. Like the United States nearly two centuries before, Kenya was organized as a republic after it gained its independence.

The ideals of democracy were not achieved. Instead of two or more opponents for president, Kenya eventually moved to a one-party system. Instead of representative democracy, members of the Kenya African National Union (KANU), took control. Kenyatta was named prime minister, then president as opposition parties joined together.

From his early work on the Nairobi municipal water board in the 1920s to his presidency in 1963, Jomo Kenyatta's political career was marked by controversy and celebration. Quitting his government job to join the Young Kikuyu Association, he was later sent to London in

1931 by the Kikuyu Central Association to meet with a parliamentary committee. He lived abroad until the mid-1940s. He held his post as president of Kenya until his death in 1978. Although he worked to craft a prosperous country that could be part of the modern world, he was also accused of fostering a system of government corruption.

Following Kenyatta's death, Vice President Daniel arap Moi became president. The country was enduring serious challenges. After becoming independent, land once owned by white settlers was purchased by the government and given in small plots to natives. Unfortunately, there was never enough land to meet demand. Worse, much of the land did not go to struggling Kenyans but went instead to people who had connections to the government. Well connected people also received most government-provided jobs. Those who tried to change this system, or spoke out against it, were jailed or deported.

In December of 2002, the first significant changes in the country's political system took place. Moi was forced by a rewritten constitution to step down after twenty-four years as president. The National

FYI FACT:

It was 10:30 a.m. on August 7, 1998, when a truck approached the United States Embassy in Nairobi, Kenya. The occupants of the truck began shooting at the guards protecting the embassy's rear gate. They threw a grenade at the guards and fled from the truck. A moment later, the truck exploded.

The explosion tore though the embassy. Over 200 died, including twelve Americans. The attack was linked to the terrorist organization al-Qaeda. In neighboring Tanzania, a simultaneous explosion at the U.S. Embassy in Dar es Salaam killed eleven more.

In June of 2011, Fazul Abdullah Mohammed, an alleged organizer of the attacks, was shot and killed in Mogadishu, Somalia.

Rainbow Coalition candidate, Mwai Kibaki, defeated the KANU candidate for the presidency.

The lives of most Kenyans were not affected by these changes. As of 2010, most lived on less than three dollars a day. One out of three adult Kenyans did not have a job. In Nairobi, the high demand for housing has led many developers to violate building codes; in June of 2011 one such structure collapsed while it was still under construction, killing several workers.

The government requires elementary-age children to attend school, but students who choose to attend high school have to pay tuition. While the Kenyan government operates many of the elementary schools, about 75 percent of schools in Kenya are community-run *Harambee* schools.

From the Swahili for "all pull together," a Harambee school is community run. It does not receive government funding.

Coffee has become one of Kenya's most important cash crops. Because of global competition, growers today earn far less than they once did.

Coffee, tea, and other agricultural products make up about half of the country's commodity exports. Yet facing competition from producers around the world, Kenyan coffee growers are unable to sell their products at the same prices as they used to.

An estimated 1,500 Kenyans died when widespread violence broke out following the 2007 presidential election. President Mwai Kibaki was reelected, but many believed that the results were rigged.

Kenyans hope that the 2010 revision to the constitution will change Kenya's future for the better. Despite the obstacles, Kenya remains a vibrant country with diverse wildlife and cultures. In the 21st century, some technological innovations have already improved the lives of the average Kenyan. For example, in 1999 when a landline was the most common type of telephone, only three out of every one hundred Kenyans owned one. Today, cell phones are common; a study released in 2012 estimates that more than 90 percent of the population now owns one.[1]

Irio

Many traditional Kenyan recipes are simple and use home-grown ingredients. A number of fruits and vegetables in Kenya were brought in by other groups—the Portuguese, for example, brought sweet potatoes, bananas, and pineapple from Brazil, while Indians brought in by the British were responsible for adding curries and spices to the national diet.

Irio is prepared by the Kikuyu tribe who grow the ingredients themselves. It is traditionally served with steak.

Ingredients:
1½   pounds potatoes, quartered
2   cups green peas
2   cups corn
2   cups red kidney beans
2   cups spinach
        Water
        Salt and Pepper

1. **With adult supervision,** put the potatoes in a large pot, cover with water, and bring to a boil. Reduce heat and simmer for 15-20 minutes until the potatoes are soft. Set them aside.
2. In a large saucepan, combine the remaining ingredients. Cook with water over low to medium heat until the vegetables are soft. Drain vegetables.
3. Mash the potatoes with a potato masher or a fork. Combine all ingredients together with a fork or wooden spoon. Season to taste with salt and pepper.

Make and Play Mankala

Mankala is a game with a long and not completely understood history. A variation of the game was played in ancient Hindu and Muslim cultures, but whether or not it was introduced to the Kenyans by Indian or Arab visitors is not known. There are different variations of the game throughout Kenya. Along the northern Kenyan coast, for example, it is called Kombe. The Maasai play a version of it with multiple players—often playing at the same time and at speeds that make it difficult to determine the rules they follow. The Maasai also call the hole where beads are dropped the "cattle corral."

Boards can be very elaborate and often are hand carved. Beads, seeds, and a variety of other objects are often used. Many children use marbles. All of these work quite well, but for this craft we will use items that are very easy to find. You will need:

One egg carton
Thirty-six playing pieces (beans, coins, beads, or stones)
Paint
Paint brush
Scissors

1. Cut the egg carton along its hinge.
2. Cut two of the wells from the top of the carton. Tape or glue one to either end of the bottom carton.
3. Paint your game board and allow it to dry.
4. Place three playing pieces each in each of the twelve cups.
   Now you're ready to play!

As this is a two-player game, place the board between the players. Each half of the carton is one player's playing space. The end cups belong to each player for storing captured pieces. Player One begins by selecting any of their six cups, removing all three pieces. Then, the player moves counter-clockwise, dropping one piece per cup. If there are pieces in the last cup where the player dropped their last piece, then those pieces are picked up. Again, one piece is dropped into each cup.

One end section belongs to Player One, the other to Player Two. When Player One reaches his or her end section, the player drops one piece into it. If it's their last piece, then they may select pieces from anywhere else on their side.

Turn ends when player drops a piece into an empty cup.

Player Two then selects pieces from his or her side of the board, and drops one each into each cup.

The game ends when one side of cups is empty. The player who has the most pieces in his or her end cup is the winner.

TIMELINE

B.C.E.

ca. 2,000,000	The first humans live in the Great Rift Valley (which includes part of Kenya).
ca. 2000-1000	Cushitic farmers and herders arrive in Kenya from other parts of Africa.
ca. 500	Bantus arrive in Kenya with iron tools for farming.

C.E.

100	By this time, trade in Kenya has been established with Arabs.
150	Ptolemy maps the coast of Kenya
ca. 632-700	The coast is settled by Arabs who develop Mombasa. Islam spreads in Kenya.
ca. 900	Mombasa is officially founded.
1498	Explorer Vasco da Gama lands on the east coast of Africa.
1505 and 1528	Portuguese attacks on Mombasa are defeated by a coalition of Swahili and Arabs.
1589	The Portuguese overwhelm the Mombasa defenders and, in 1593, establish Fort Jesus to defend the region.
1660	Omanis attack Mombasa.
1729	Omanis gain control of Mombasa, overthrowing the Portuguese.
1849	German missionaries are the first Europeans to see the snow-capped mountains in Kenya's interior.
1883-1884	Scottish explorer Joseph Thomson explores Mount Kilimanjaro and Mount Kenya along with the eastern portions of Lake Victoria. He publishes his account in the book *Through Masai Land.*
1887	In May, the British East Africa Association signs a fifty-year lease for the region including Kenya.
1895	The British government takes over development and forms the East Africa Protectorate.
Early 1900s	A railway constructed from Mombasa to Lake Victoria by the East Africa Protectorate allows white settlers to move into the highlands.
1907	The Legislative Council, made up of British settlers, holds its first meeting.
1920	East Africa Protectorate becomes the Kenya Colony and Protectorate, run by a British governor.
1921	The Young Kikuyu Association is formed to represent the interests of native Kenyans.
1939	World War II begins.
1942	Kenyan African Union (KAU) formed to campaign for Kenyan political rights and independence.
1947	Jomo Kenyatta becomes KAU leader.
1952	The Mau Mau begin a violent campaign against British supporters. State of emergency is declared, and Kenyatta is arrested.
1956	Mau Mau rebellion crushed after the deaths of thousands.
1959	Louis and Mary Leakey discover portions of a 1.75 million-year-old skull in Olduvai Gorge, south of the Kenya-Tanzania border.
1963	Kenya gains independence, with Kenyatta as prime minister.
1964	Republic of Kenya formed. Kenyatta becomes president and Jaramogi Oginga Odinga vice-president.

1969	Richard Leakey, the son of Louis and Mary, discovers chopping tools and the partial skull of an australopithecine near Lake Turkana.
1978	Kenyatta dies in office, and is succeeded by Vice-President Daniel arap Moi.
1984	Kamoya Kimeu, a longtime Leakey collaborator, discovers a nearly complete 1.6 million-year-old skeleton.
1998	The August bombing of the U.S. Embassy in Nairobi kills over 200 people; it is believed to be the work of al-Qaeda.
1999	Richard Leakey appointed to the Kenyan Civil Service in fight against governmental corruption.
2002	Mwai Kibaki becomes president, ending KANU's neary forty years in power.
2005	A new constitution is written following violent protests in Nairobi over the power of the president; voters reject new constitution.
2006	A drought in Kenya leaves 3.5 million northern Kenyans in need of food aid.
2007	In December, disputed presidential elections lead to widespread violence which results in the deaths of an estimated 1,500 Kenyans.
2010	A new constitution reduces presidential power.
2012	Oil is discovered in the northwest of Kenya.

GLOSSARY

anthropology (an-thra-POL-uh-jee): The study of human beings and their ancestors.

arid (AIR-id): Very dry; not having enough rainfall for farming.

expatriate (ex-PAY-tree-eyt): Citizen of one country who lives full time in another.

fossil (FAHS-uhll): The remains or impression of a living creature preserved in the earth's crust.

monsoon (mohn-SOON): A periodic wind in the Indian Ocean which usually brings heavy rain.

paleoanthropology (pay-lee-oh-an-thruh-POL-uh-jee): Branch of anthropology dealing with human ancestors and the study of their fossils.

paleontology (pay-lee-uhn-TALL-uh-jee): Science focused on studying ancient life using fossils.

republic (ree-PUB-lik): Government whose chief of state is not a monarch; the greatest power rests with its citizens who vote for their representatives.

savanna (suh-VAN-uh): Tropical or subtropical grasslands with few trees.

vegetarian (vej-ih-TAIR-ee-uhn): One who does not eat meat.

Chapter 3. The Human Cradle

1. *Time,* "Puzzling Out Man's Ascent," November 7, 1977.

2. Ira Flatow, *Science Friday,* "Richard Leakey Reflects On Human Past—And Future," National Public Radio, April 15, 2011. http://www.npr.org/2011/04/15/135442954/richard-leakey-reflects-on-human-past-and-future

3. John Reader, *Africa* (Washington, D.C.: National Geographic Society, 2001), p. 29.

4. Ibid., p. 29.

5. John Noble Wilford, *The New York Times*, "Tracking Lineage Through a Bramble," May 10, 2011, p. D1(L).

6. Ira Flatow, *Science Friday,* "Richard Leakey Reflects On Human Past—And Future," National Public Radio, April 15, 2011. http://www.npr.org/2011/04/15/135442954/richard-leakey-reflects-on-human-past-and-future

Chapter 4. Marathons Around Mount Kenya

1. James Waindi, *[Nairobi] Standard,* "Boston Marathon winner urges IAAF to certify his time as new world record," April 21, 2011. http://www.standardmedia.co.ke/sports/InsidePage.php?id=2000033719&cid=39&story=Boston%20Marathon%20winner%20urges%20IAAF%20to%20certify%20his%20time%20as%20new%20world%20

2. MarathonGuide.com, "All Time Best Men's Marathon Times." http://www.marathonguide.com/history/records/alltimelist.cfm?Gen=M&Sort=Country

3. Agence France-Presse, "Controversial Danish Research Claims to Explain African Running Dominance," November 26, 2000.

Chapter 5. Migrations Along the Rift

1. Richard B. Lee and Robert K. Hitchcock, *African Study Monographs,* "African Hunter-Gatherers: Survival, History and the Politics of Identity," March 2001, pp. 257-280.

Chapter 6. Mombasa: The Place of War

1. John Reader, *Africa* (Washington, D.C.: National Geographic Society, 2001), p. 70.

Chapter 7. Colonized

1. Gerald Herbert Portal, "Mombasa-Uganda Route," *Reports Relating to Uganda* (London: Edward Arnold, 1894), p. 3.

Chapter 8. Independence!

1. Robert Hahn and Peter Passell, *U.S. News,* "How Cell Phones Are Boosting Kenya's Economy," April 12, 2012. http://www.usnews.com/opinion/blogs/economic-intelligence/2012/04/12/how-cell-phones-are-boosting-kenyas-economy

Books

Broberg, Catherine. *Kenya in Pictures.* Minneapolis: Lerner Publications Co., 2003.

Giles, Bridget. *Kenya.* Washington, D.C.: National Geographic Society, 2006.

McNair, Sylvia, and Lynne Mansure. *Kenya.* New York: Children's Press, 2002.

Nivola, Claire A. *Planting the Trees of Kenya: The Story of Wangari Maathai.* New York: Farrar, Straus, and Giroux, 2008.

Parkinson, Tom, et. al. *Lonely Planet Guide: Kenya.* Berkeley, CA: Lonely Planet Publications, 2006.

Russ, Larry. *The Complete Mancala Games Book.* New York: Marlowe & Company, 2000.

Trillo, Richard. *The Rough Guide to Kenya.* London: Rough Guides, 2010.

On the Internet

African Wildlife Foundation: "Colobus Monkey"
  http://www.awf.org/content/wildlife/detail/colobusmonkey

Archaeologyinfo.com: "Human Evolution: A Description of Fossil Hominids and Their Origins"
  http://archaeologyinfo.com/human-evolution/

BBC News Africa: "Kenya Profile"
  http://news.bbc.co.uk/2/hi/africa/country_profiles/1024563.stm#facts

Kenya Birds: "Birding in Kenya"
  http://www.kenyabirds.org.uk/

National Geographic: "Kenya Travel Guide"
  http://travel.nationalgeographic.com/travel/countries/kenya-guide/

U.S. Department of State: "Kenya"
  http://www.state.gov/r/pa/ei/bgn/2962.htm

WORKS CONSULTED

Barcott, Rye. *It Happened On the Way to War: A Marine's Path to Peace.* New York: Bloomsbury USA, 2010.

"Controversial Danish Research claims to explain African Running Dominance." Agence France-Presse, November 26, 2000.

Flatow, Ira. "Richard Leakey Reflects On Human Past—And Future," *Science Friday,* National Public Radio, April 15, 2011. http://www.npr.org/2011/04/15/135442954/richard-leakey-reflects-on-human-past-and-future

Hahn, Robert, and Peter Passell. "How Cell Phones Are Boosting Kenya's Economy." *U.S. News,* April 12, 2012. http://www.usnews.com/opinion/blogs/economic-intelligence/2012/04/12/how-cell-phones-are-boosting-kenyas-economy

High Altitude Training Centre—Iten, Kenya
http://www.lornah.com/

Huxley, Elspeth Joscelin Grant. *Out in the Midday Sun: My Kenya*. New York, NY: Viking, 1987.

JamboKenya, "The Rift Valley,"
http://www.jambokenya.com/jambo/location/rvalley.htm

"Kenya." *Destination Africa*. Dir. David Lionel. Education 2000, Inc., 1988, 2005. DVD.

Lee, Richard B., and Robert K. Hitchcock. "African Hunter-Gatherers: Survival, History and the Politics of Identity." *African Study Monographs,* March 2001. pp. 257-280.

MarathonGuide.com, "All Time Best Men's Marathon Times," http://www.marathonguide.com/history/records/alltimelist.cfm?Gen=M&Sort=Country

National Museums of Kenya
http://www.museums.or.ke/

Pavitt, Nigel. *Kenya: A Country in the Making, 1880-1940*. New York: W.W. Norton & Co., 2008.

PBS, "Running," *Frontline/World*,
http://www.pbs.org/frontlineworld/stories/kenya/facts.html

Plate Tectonics, "The Great Rift Valley will Lead to the Somali Plate,"
http://www.platetectonics.com/oceanfloors/somali.asp

Portal, Gerald Herbert, et. al. "Mombasa-Uganda Route." *Reports Relating to Uganda*. London: Edward Arnold, 1894.

"Puzzling Out Man's Ascent." *Time,* November 7, 1977. http://205.188.238.109/time/magazine/article/0,9171,947970-1,00.html

Reader, John. *Africa*. Washington, D.C.: National Geographic Society, 2001.

Trillo, Richard. *The Rough Guide to Kenya*. London: Rough Guides, 2010.

Visonà, Monica Blackmun. *A History of Art in Africa*. New York: Harry N. Abrams, 2001.

Waindi, James. "Boston Marathon winner urges IAAF to certify his time as new world record." *[Nairobi] Standard,* April 21, 2011. http://www.standardmedia.co.ke/sports/InsidePage.php?id=2000033719&cid=39&story=Boston%20Marathon%20winner%20urges%20IAAF%20to%20certify%20his%20time%20as%20new%20world%20

Wilford, John Noble. "Tracking lineage through a bramble." *The New York Times,* May 10, 2011, p. D1(L).

Born in Boston, Massachusetts, John Bankston began writing articles while still a teenager. Since then, over 200 of his articles have been published in magazines and newspapers across the country, including travel articles in *The Tallahassee Democrat*, *The Orlando Sentinel*, and *The Tallahassean*. He is the author of over sixty biographies for young adults, including works on Alexander the Great, scientist Stephen Hawking, author F. Scott Fitzgerald, and actor Jodi Foster. At sixteen he enjoyed his first experience with overseas adventure, visiting Italy for two weeks with his sophomore Latin class. He currently lives in Newport Beach, California.